DOCKSIDE

STAGE
5
BOOK 3

CYCLE RIDE

John Townsend

RISING★STARS

It was a warm, sunny day and Oz had plans at Club OK. He called, "Hey, you guys! How about going on a bike ride?"

"I haven't got a bike," Asad said.
"We've got a couple of spare bikes here if you want," Miss Evans said.

3

"Where will we cycle?" Jack asked.
"I can't be late back. I've got to go
to my uncle's wedding."

4

Oz held bits of paper. "How long you take is up to you. I thought you might like to have a go at a quiz. It's like a treasure hunt."

Oz and Miss Evans set off first so they could hide clues along the way. Halim and Caleb rode side by side. Maya laughed, "I thought I was seeing double with you two like that!"

CLUE NUMBER 1

I am an insect.
You can sit in me.

"It's a gamble but I think I know where to go," Maya said. She rode off, with Halim close behind.

Maya went to the children's playground. "I was right," she smiled. "The next clue is in this bee."

CLUE NUMBER 2

9

Jack and Asad were stuck on the first clue. "It says we have to look for something like an insect that we can sit in," Asad said.

"Aha!" Jack yelled. "Look, a VW Beetle! A beetle is an insect and we can sit in the car. We found it!"
An old car was in a patch of weeds.

"Do you think we should be sitting in this? Where's the next clue?" Asad asked.
"My uncle's car is just like this old car." Jack chuckled and beeped the horn.

The man looked angry.

Later …

"That VW Beetle has given me an idea," said Jack.
"Oh no," Asad groaned.

"My uncle's car is just like it," Jack went on.
"It'll be parked at the hotel for his wedding.
Let's cycle there and make a bit of trouble!"

"Here's my uncle's car," Jack said.
"Let's do it up with loo rolls and stuff.
We can stick bits all over, at every angle."